VOCAL SELECTIONS

Zorbá

Lyrics by **FRED EBB**   Music by **JOHN KANDER**

CONTENTS

ISBN 0-7935-3298-1

HAL•LEONARD®
CORPORATION

7777 W. BLUEMOUND RD. P.O. BOX 13819 MILWAUKEE, WI 53213

For all works contained herein:
Unauthorized copying, arranging, adapting, recording or public performance is an infringement of copyright.
Infringers are liable under the law.

Visit Hal Leonard Online at
www.halleonard.com

ZORBÁ THEME
(Life Is)

Lyrics by
FRED EBB

Music by
JOHN KANDER

Copyright © 1968 by Alley Music Corp. and Trio Music Company, Inc.
Copyright Renewed
International Copyright Secured   All Rights Reserved
Used by Permission

Life is where you wait while you're wait-ing to leave.

Life is where you grin _____ and grieve. _____

Hav-ing if you're luck-y, want-ing if you're not.

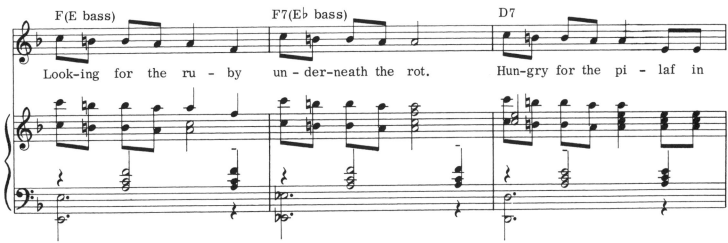

Look-ing for the ru-by un-der-neath the rot. Hun-gry for the pi-laf in

some-one else-'s pot but that's the on - ly choice you've

got! Life is where you stand just be - fore you are flat.

Life is on - ly that, Mis - ter, Life is simp-ly that, Mis - ter,

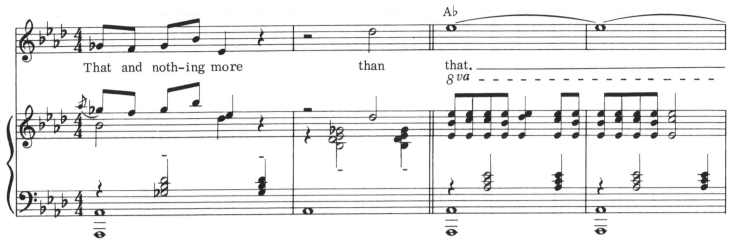

That and noth-ing more   than   that. _____

Life is what you feel   till you

can't feel at all.   Life is where you fly _____ and

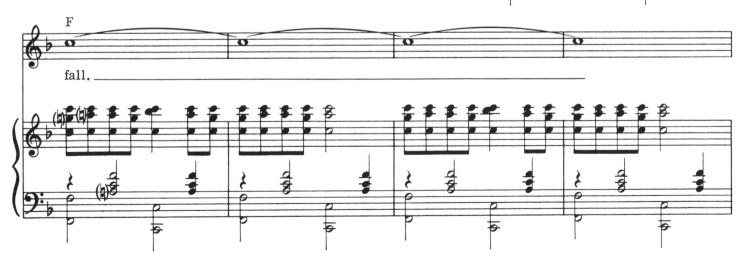

fall. _____

Run-ning for the shel-ter nak-ed in the snow, Learn-ing that a tear drops

an-y-where you go. Find-ing it's the mud that makes the ros-es grow. But

that's the on-ly choice you know.

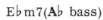

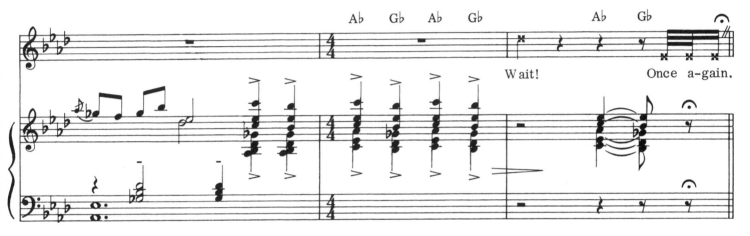

Life is what you do while you're wait-ing to die.

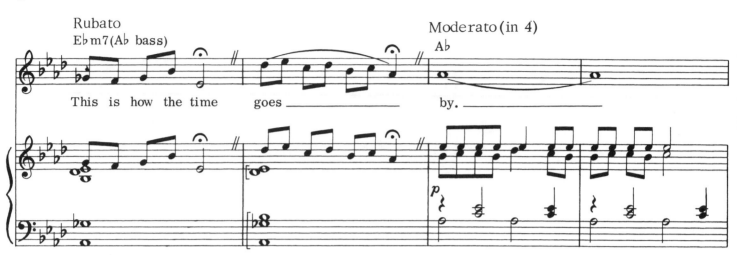

This is how the time goes _____ by. _____

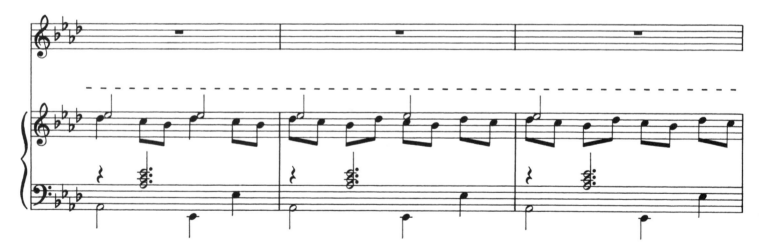

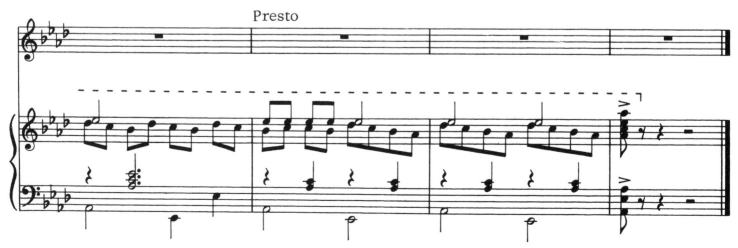

HAPPY BIRTHDAY TO ME

Lyrics by
FRED EBB

Music by
JOHN KANDER

Copyright © 1968 by Alley Music Corp. and Trio Music Company, Inc.
Copyright Renewed
International Copyright Secured All Rights Reserved
Used by Permission

NO BOOM BOOM

Lyrics by
FRED EBB

Music by
JOHN KANDER

Copyright © 1968 by Alley Music Corp. and Trio Music Company, Inc.
Copyright Renewed
International Copyright Secured   All Rights Reserved
Used by Permission

wide plumed hats and gold-en braid and pa-tent leath-er shoes.___ They were

just a-bout to fire___ on Crete when on my knees in a pink chem-ise I dis-

tract-ed them toute suite, by say - ing Please sir, lit-tle

Ad-mir-al, no boom boom. Please sir, pret-ty

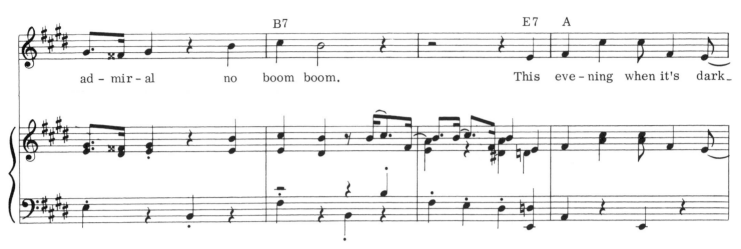

ad - mir - al no boom boom. This eve - ning when it's dark

I'll let you come to my room but first you have to

prom - ise, no boom boom. My French-man smelled of

le - mon, My I - tal - ian vi - o - let. My Eng - lish smelled of

some-thing I for-get. My Rus-sian wore a musk_

_ they make from oil - y Geor-gian bark. I learned each smell so

I could tell be-tween them in the dark. They'd fill a bath with

pink cham-pagne,_ then throw me in the tub_ While two would drink, the

oth-er two would scrub. We played that way un-

til the day__ they set this is - land free. And so, my dear, if

Crete's still here, it's all be-cause of me. It was I __ who kept the nav - y

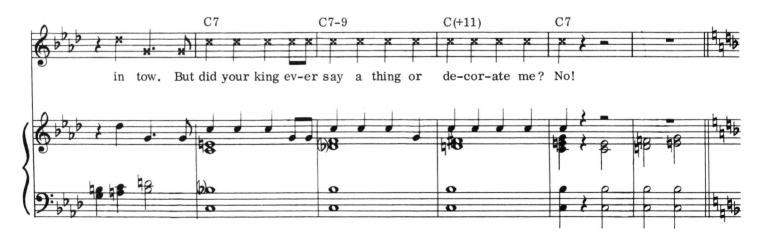

in tow. But did your king ev-er say a thing or de-cor-ate me? No!

ONLY LOVE

Lyrics by
FRED EBB

Music by
JOHN KANDER

Copyright © 1968 by Alley Music Corp. and Trio Music Company, Inc.
Copyright Renewed
International Copyright Secured   All Rights Reserved
Used by Permission

So give me love on-ly love _____ That's ev-'ry-thing.

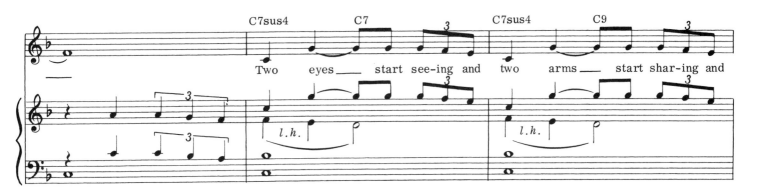

Two eyes ____ start see-ing and two arms ____ start shar-ing and

two lips ____ start know-ing how good it is. _____ To feel,

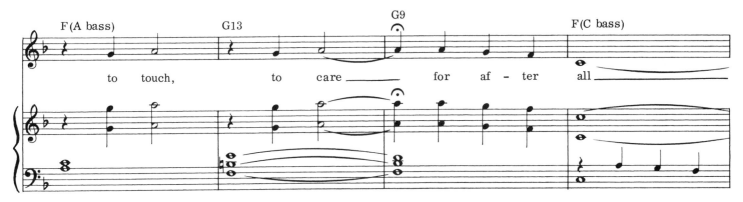

to touch, to care _____ for af - ter all _____

af - ter love _____ what else is there? _____

THE TOP OF THE HILL

Lyrics by
FRED EBB

Music by
JOHN KANDER

Copyright © 1968 by Alley Music Corp. and Trio Music Company, Inc.
Copyright Renewed
International Copyright Secured   All Rights Reserved
Used by Permission

Tempo (Allegro moderato)

waiting for you _____ waiting for you ____

There's a door to the room in a house at the top of the hill _____ where some-one's wait-ing for you _____

wait-ing for you! _____ There's a wom-an at the door! _____ There's a

wom-an at the door!_____ To the

room in a house at the top of the hill_____ wait-ing for

you. _____

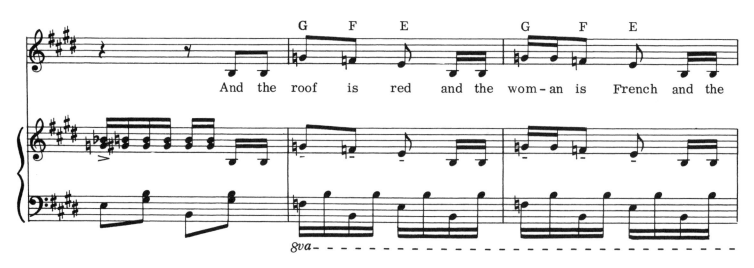

And the roof is red and the wom-an is French and the

bed is hard and the sheet is rough and the bread is old and the

wine is hot and the night is cold but the wom-an is not at the

house at the top of the hill! _____

_____ There's a house at the top of the

door to the room in a house at the top of the hill ____

____ where some - one's wait - ing for you. ____

Wait - ing for you. ____ There's a wom-an at the door

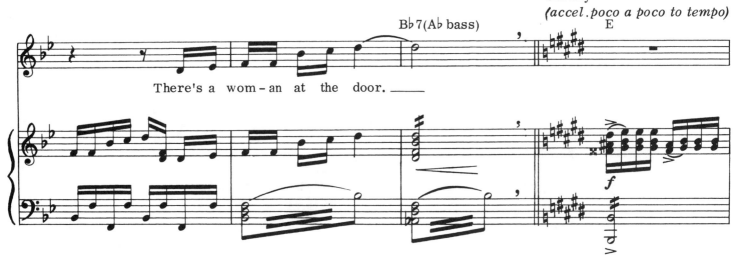

There's a wom-an at the door. ____

There's a house at the top of the hill. There's a

house at the top of the hill _____ where

some - one's wait-ing for you   Wait - ing for you. ___

THE FIRST TIME

Lyrics by
FRED EBB

Music by
JOHN KANDER

Copyright © 1968 by Alley Music Corp. and Trio Music Company, Inc.
Copyright Renewed
International Copyright Secured   All Rights Reserved
Used by Permission

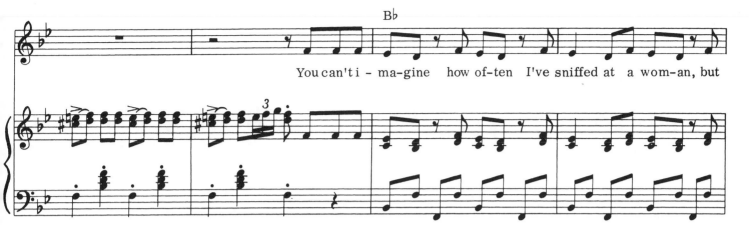

You can't i-ma-gine how of-ten I've sniffed at a wom-an, but

each time _____ is the first time. _____ I

pound on a ta-ble. I jump on a chair. I crawl up a moun-tain to

breathe in the air. By now I've stopped count-ing how of - ten I've been there, but

each time _____ is the first time. _____

I look at a flow-er I stick my nose in, or stare at, or

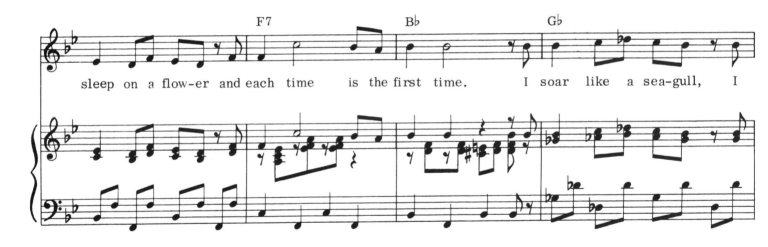

sleep on a flow-er and each time is the first time. I soar like a sea-gull, I

stamp like a bull. I comb out my whis-kers for la-dies to pull. I

I AM FREE

Lyrics by
FRED EBB

Music by
JOHN KANDER

Copyright © 1968 by Alley Music Corp. and Trio Music Company, Inc.
Copyright Renewed
International Copyright Secured   All Rights Reserved
Used by Permission

ask noth-ing! I judge noth-ing! I am free!_____ There's

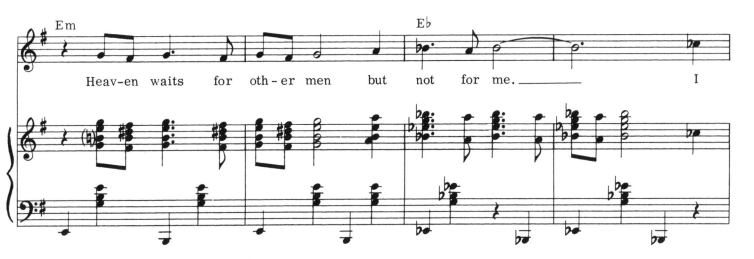

one Zor-ba! But that Zor-ba! I must be!_____

Heav-en waits for oth-er men but not for me._____ I

fear noth-ing!_____ I hope for noth-ing!_____

I am free.

D7sus4 (no F♯)

(Spoken:)

(Zorba:) Hey boss! Do you want to hear a story? *(Nikos:) Yes.*

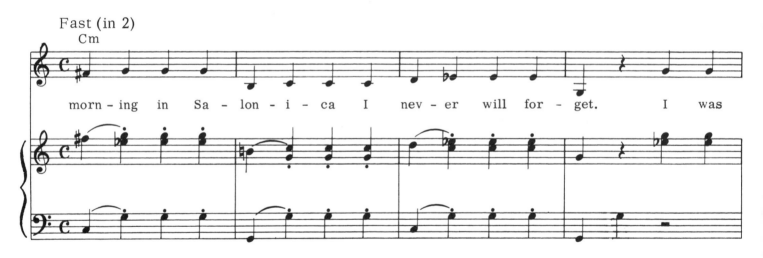

(Zorba:) What did you say? *(Nikos:) Yes, I want to hear a story.* *(Zorba:) You do?* *(Zorba:) Then I'll tell you*

One

Fast (in 2)

Cm

morn - ing in Sa - lon - i - ca I nev - er will for - get. I was

pass - ing by the old - est man that I had ev - er met. He was

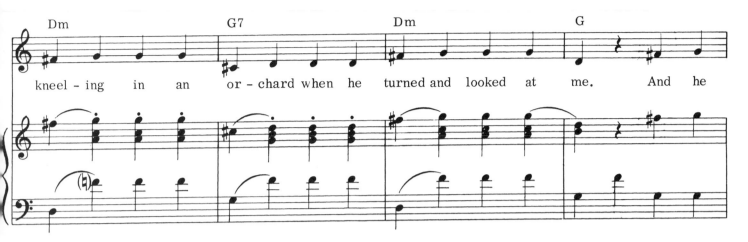

kneel - ing in an or - chard when he turned and looked at me. And he

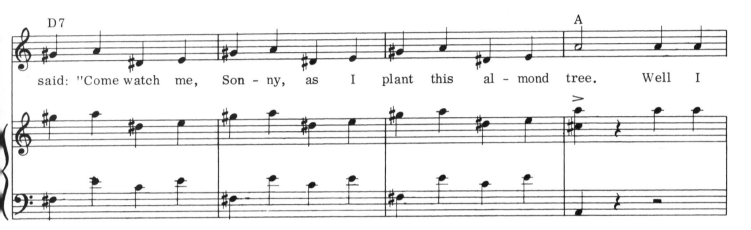

said: "Come watch me, Son - ny, as I plant this al - mond tree. Well I

tell you boss that fel - la he was o - ver nine - ty - five. And I

think he had a week or may - be two to stay a - live. But he

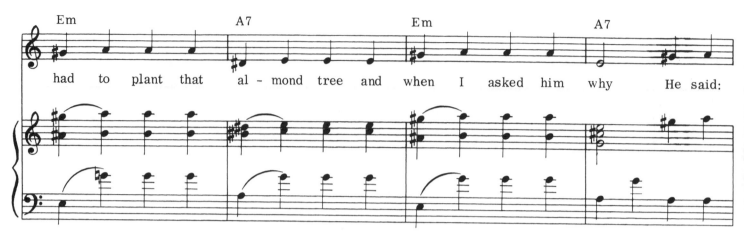

had to plant that al - mond tree and when I asked him why He said:

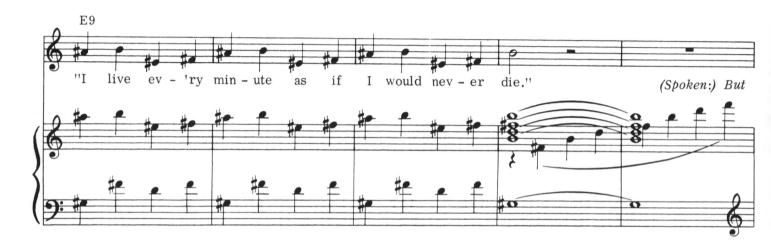

"I live ev - 'ry min - ute as if I would nev - er die." *(Spoken:)* But

isn't that something boss? He lived as if he would never die. I live as if I'd die

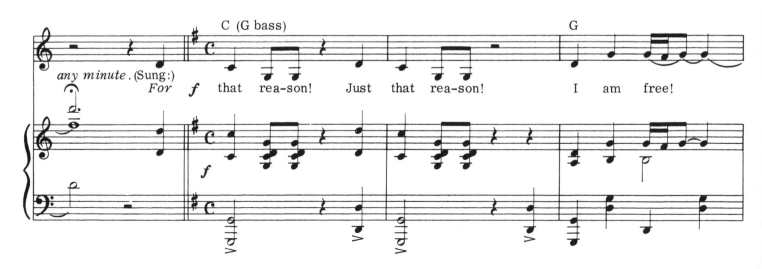

any minute. (Sung:) For *f* that rea - son! Just that rea - son! I am free!

I see some-where! I go some-where! I am free!

Think of that when-ev-er you re-mem-ber me _____ I

fear noth-ing _____ I hope for noth-ing! _____

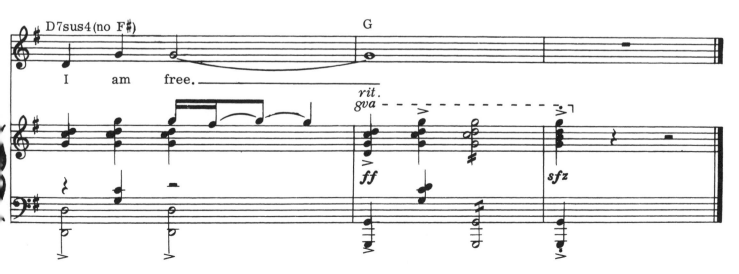

I am free. _____

WHY CAN'T I SPEAK

Lyrics by
FRED EBB

Music by
JOHN KANDER

Copyright © 1968 by Alley Music Corp. and Trio Music Company, Inc.
Copyright Renewed
International Copyright Secured   All Rights Reserved
Used by Permission

B♭(D bass) C13 B♭(F bass)

Why can't I say it? Let out the feel-ing When we're to-geth-er

E♭ (F bass)

Why won't the words come? Why can't I speak?

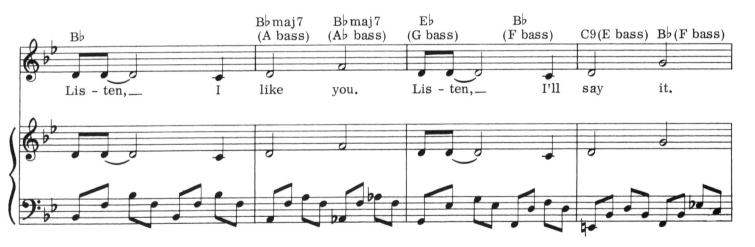

B♭   B♭maj7 (A bass) B♭maj7 (A♭ bass) E♭ (G bass) B♭ (F bass) C9(E bass) B♭(F bass)

Lis-ten,__ I like you. Lis-ten,__ I'll say it.

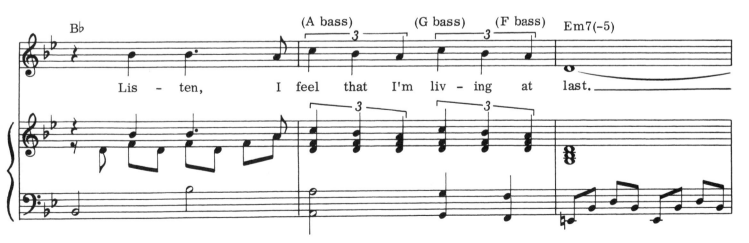

B♭   (A bass) (G bass) (F bass) Em7(-5)

Lis-ten, I feel that I'm liv-ing at last.___

Lis - ten, I'll be good to you   Lis - ten, I'll take

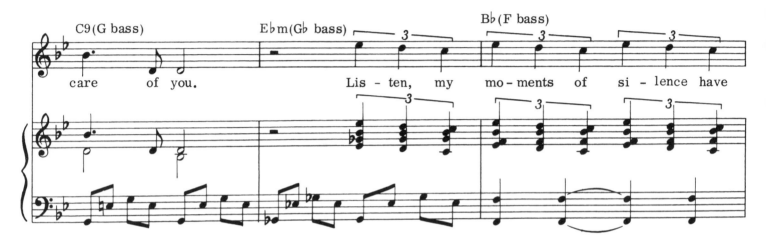

care of you.   Lis - ten, my mo - ments of si - lence have

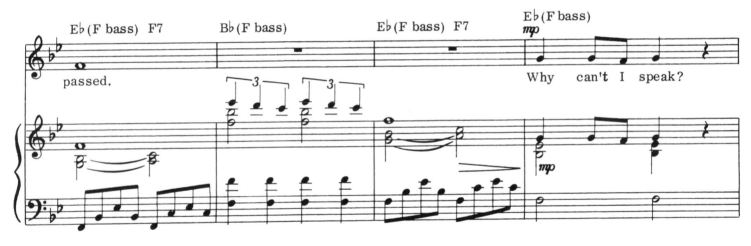

passed.   Why can't I speak?

Why can't I speak?